Formula E

Thomas Kingsley Troupe

 45th Parallel Press

Published in the United States of America by Cherry Lake Publishing Group
Ann Arbor, Michigan
www.cherrylakepublishing.com

Reading Adviser: Beth Walker Gambro, MS, Ed., Reading Consultant, Yorkville, IL

PHOTOS CREDITS:
www.shutterstock.com : cover ©Oskar SCHULER, page 2 ©Jens Mommens, page 4-5 ©Jens Mommens, page 5 ©EvrenKalinbacak, page 6-7 ©Cineberg, page 7 ©AlessioDeMarco, page 8 ©duncan1890, page 9 ©Darren Brode, page 10 ©Jay Hirano, page 11 © Racing © Sharkphoto l Dreamstime.com, page 12 ©ABB/Formula e (fiaFormulae.com), page 13 ©Sam Bloxham/LAT/Formula E(fiaFormulae.com), page 14 ©Christopher Lyzcen, page 14 ©Rawpixel.com, page 15 ©Jens Mommens, page 16 © Vincent Huybrechts, page 17 ©Malcolm Griffiths/LAT Images (fiaFormulae.com) page 18© Marco Iacobucci Epp, page 18 map ©google earth, page 19 ©Jens Mommens, page20 © Marco Iacobucci Epp, page 21©Jens Mommens, page 22 ©Giorgio Rossi, page 22 ©Marco Iacobucci Epp, page 23 ©Photo by Simon Galloway /LAT Images (fiaFormulae.com), page 24© shutterstock.com/Cineberg, page 25© AstroVictor, page 26©Sam Bagnall (fiaFormulae.com), page 27 ©Simon Galloway (fiaFormulae.com), page 28 Jens Mommens, page 29 ©Sam Bagnall, page 31 ©Sam Bagnall (fiaFormulae.com)

Produced for Cherry Lake Publishing by bluedooreducation.com

Copyright © 2026 by Cherry Lake Publishing Group

All rights reserved. No part of this book may be reproduced or utilized in any form or by any means without written permission from the publisher.

45th Parallel Press is an imprint of Cherry Lake Publishing Group.

Library of Congress Cataloging-in-Publication Data has been filed and is available at catalog.loc.gov.
Printed in the United States of America

Note from Publisher: Websites change regularly, and their future contents are outside of our control. Supervise children when conducting any recommended online searches for extended learning opportunities.

ABOUT THE AUTHOR
Thomas Kingsley Troupe is the author of over 300 books for young readers. When he's not writing, he enjoys reading, playing video games, and hunting ghosts as part of the Twin Cities Paranormal Society. Otherwise, he's probably taking a nap or something. TKT lives in Woodbury, MN, with his two sons.

Table of Contents

CHAPTER 1
Introduction... 4

CHAPTER 2
Formula E History 8

CHAPTER 3
Formula E Events 14

CHAPTER 4
Formula E Vehicles 20

CHAPTER 5
Formula E Drivers 26

Did You Know? 30
Find Out More 32
Glossary 32
Index 32

Chapter 1
Introduction

The race cars slowly and quietly pull up. They get into position. They're all waiting behind the starting line. Drivers pull into their spots. They are numbered 1 through 20. Driver 12 looks at the cars ahead. They're all ready to go. Their engines hum.

The lights above the starting line light up. Red, red, red, red…green! The race is on! The crowd cheers as the cars zip off. There isn't loud revving. The racers' vehicles sound like remote control cars. They are moving at top speed almost instantly. The crowd goes wild!

Starting-line lights tell drivers when to go.

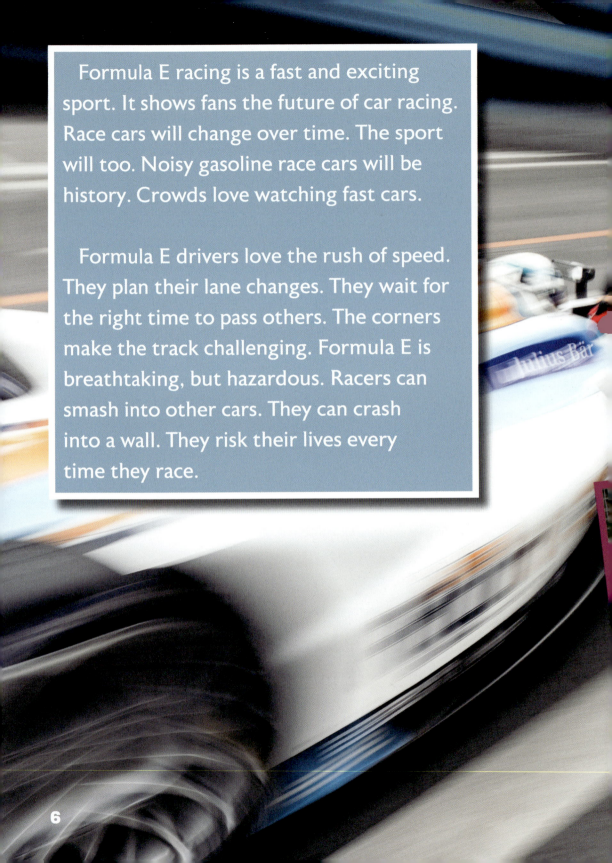

Formula E racing is a fast and exciting sport. It shows fans the future of car racing. Race cars will change over time. The sport will too. Noisy gasoline race cars will be history. Crowds love watching fast cars.

Formula E drivers love the rush of speed. They plan their lane changes. They wait for the right time to pass others. The corners make the track challenging. Formula E is breathtaking, but hazardous. Racers can smash into other cars. They can crash into a wall. They risk their lives every time they race.

Formula E is not for people who like to move slow. Is the action worth the risk? Let's learn more!

Formula E describes the type of race car. They are single seat, high-speed, racing vehicles. They run completely on battery power. The "E" stands for electric.

Chapter 2

Formula E History

Formula E racing is a very new sport. Electric cars are not that new. The first electric car was built in the 1830s. It wasn't very successful. Throughout the years, car companies wanted them to work. The technology wasn't ready. Batteries couldn't be recharged like they can today. Cars powered with gasoline became popular.

An illustration of a man driving an early electric-powered motorcar in the 1890s

An electric car from the early 1900s

Electric cars were difficult to make work. They were heavy. They were twice as expensive as gas cars. They didn't drive as fast as gas cars. They didn't go as far as gas cars. Inventors still kept trying. It took decades for Formula E cars to reach the racetrack.

Robert Anderson lived in Scotland. He built the first electric car. It happened between 1832 and 1839. His car looked like a carriage without horses. His idea is almost 200 years old. It still inspires electric car makers today.

Formula E sport was modeled after Formula 1 racing. It would have one big difference. Its cars wouldn't run on gasoline. All of its race cars would be electric.

This Formula 1 car looks similar to a Formula E car. However, this car runs on gasoline.

The first Formula E race season was 2014/2015. It started in Beijing, China, on the Olympic Park grounds. Twenty cars raced that day. They featured racers from around the world.

The racers did 25 laps around the course. Halfway through the race, the drivers had to stop. The batteries couldn't last the whole time.

The first racers were called Gen 1 cars. They were used for the 2014/2015 season.

The drivers had to jump out of their first cars. They finished the race in a charged backup racer.

A driver climbs into a new, fully charged car.

Chapter 3

Formula E Events

Formula E races are a lot like most races. Racers compete on a track. The track is different for each location. They are set up on city streets. This brings the race closer to people. Racers face off before the actual race. They do a series of **qualifying** races. Qualifying means testing for skill. These tests mean only the best move on to the main event.

Digital timers are used to keep a racer's time within a fraction of a second.

There are 11 Formula E teams. Each team has 2 drivers. These are the 2 drivers with the fastest qualifying time races. Some teams can have 2 drivers in the same race! Formula E races used to be 45 minutes long. Drivers would complete between 33 and 46 laps per race. In 2023, the rules changed. Now racers need to complete 33 laps.

Formula E cars drive fast. The cars can reach speeds of 173 miles (280 kilometers) per hour. They go from 0-62 miles (100 km) per hour in 2.8 seconds. They are not as fast as Formula 1 cars. At least, not yet.

Attack Mode is used in races. There are special spots on the track. When a car drives over it, it adds power. The driver can use the power boost for a limited time.

The new Formula E cars have a lot of power.

The biggest Formula E race is held every year. It is called the *ABB FIA Formula E World Championship*. Races are held around the world. A popular course is in Monaco. It has 19 turns on the track. There are hills to make the race challenging.

The race track at Monaco.

Formula E teams earn points during the season. They get points for winning and for fastest lap. There are even points for getting **pole position**. The pole position is at the front of the starting grid, on the inside of the front row. Drivers have to earn this position. It is usually the best starting position.

Chapter 4
Formula E Vehicles

Electric cars are always changing. People design faster and better cars. Soon they will be as fast or faster than Formula 1 cars. The sport has already seen progress. The first Gen 1 racers lacked battery power. Inventors went to work on that problem.

Four years later, Gen 2 cars arrived. They could race twice the distance. Drivers didn't have to switch cars. In 2022, Gen 3 cars were introduced. They were lighter and faster than Gen 2 cars. They increased in power by 100 **kilowatts.** This is the measurement used for determining electrical power.

All Formula E teams must use the same car models. This keeps competition fair. The car's **chassis**, the main frame of the car, can't be changed. They can't **modify**, or change, the battery. They all use tires made from natural rubber and recycled fibers. Formula E races try to keep the planet green!

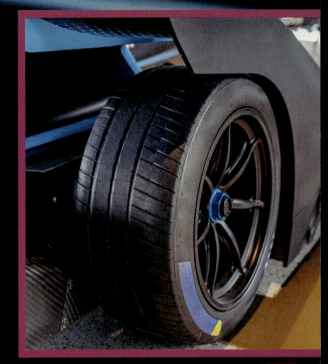

The teams are allowed to make some changes. Sometimes they use different software. It helps the car's performance. It can balance where the battery's power goes. The right software makes a huge difference on race day.

The Formula E steering wheel looks like a video game controller. A main screen shows important information. The driver can see speed and battery **status**, or how much battery power is left. The screen also shows tire pressure, brake temperature, and more.

The steering wheel has switches and paddles. The switches can shift power to front and rear brakes. The paddles can give the cars a lift. This helps them ease and coast into turns.

The blue button turns on the radio. It is not for music! The radio lets the driver communicate with their team.

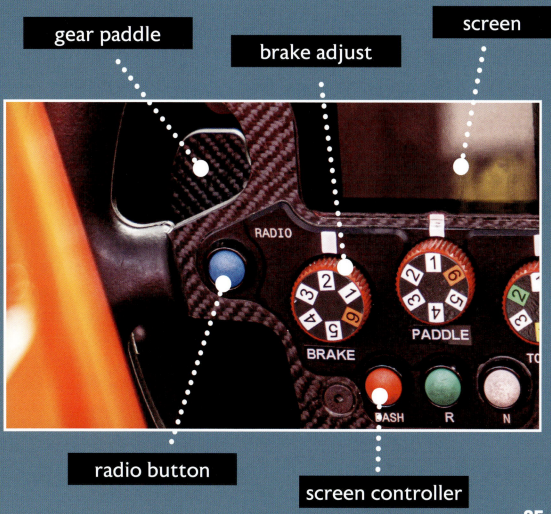

gear paddle
brake adjust
screen
radio button
screen controller

Chapter 5
Formula E Drivers

Formula E drivers wear racing suits like other race car drivers. They are made with **flame-resistant** material. Flame-resistant means protects against fire. They also wear helmets with visors. The helmets allow the drivers to talk to their crew. Drivers wear racing gloves too.

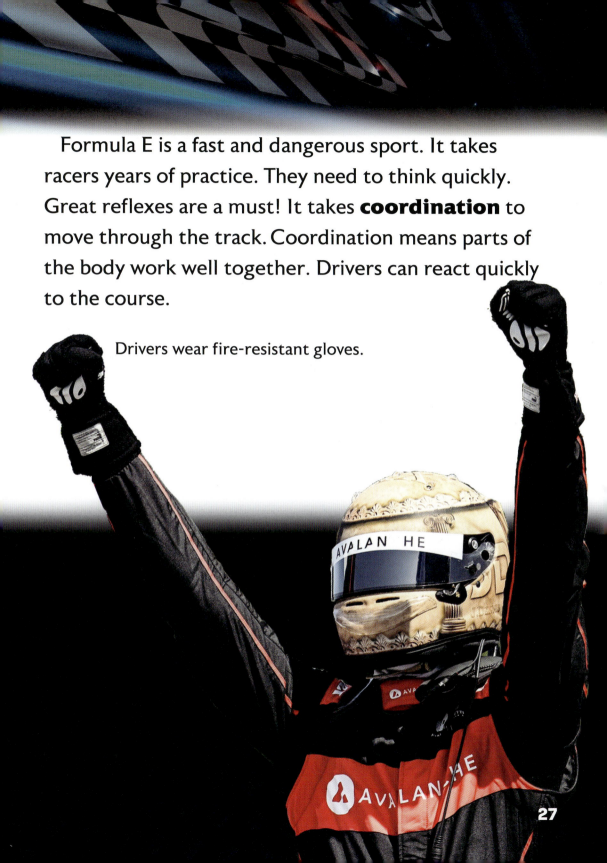

Formula E is a fast and dangerous sport. It takes racers years of practice. They need to think quickly. Great reflexes are a must! It takes **coordination** to move through the track. Coordination means parts of the body work well together. Drivers can react quickly to the course.

Drivers wear fire-resistant gloves.

Formula E proves races don't need to be loud! It is a speedy and awesome sport. Crowds love seeing the fast action. Drivers race to rule the track.

Formula E will change over the years. New cars will be made. New tracks will be built. The fight for first place will get even more exciting.

Are you ready to watch it happen? See if there's a Formula E event happening near you. Watch the sport for yourself. Off to the races!

Did You Know?

Formula E vehicles are made up of many parts. The parts are made of different materials. Carbon fiber, metals, and even the rubber tires are important materials for the car.

chassis: made of lightweight carbon-fiber composite

driver seat: an aluminum tub with a titanium bar called a halo over the top for crash protection

steering wheel: has controls to adjust power and a screen to see the car's battery power level and speed

tires: designed to last the entire race without being changed and help extend the car's battery life

battery pack: located behind the driver and can last for 30 to 40 laps

electric motor: located behind the driver and has a part that charges the battery whenever the driver uses the brakes

spoilers: parts of the front and back of the car that help direct airflow and make the car move more quickly

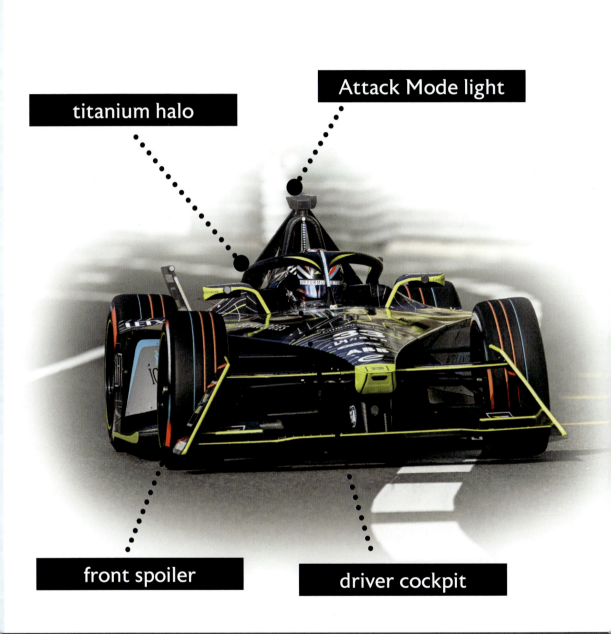

Find Out More

BOOKS
Rule, Heather. *Formula One Racing Cars*. Minneapolis, MN: Abdo Publishing, 2024.

Worms, Penny. *Race Cars*. Mankato, MN: Black Rabbit Books, 2016.

WEBSITES
Search these online sources with an adult:

Anatomy of a Formula E steering wheel | FIA Formula E

Formula E Facts | National Geographic Kids

Glossary

chassis (CHAS-ee) the base frame of a motor vehicle

coordination (koh-or-duh-NAY-shuhn) ability to use different body parts to complete a task easily

flame-resistant (FLAYM rih-ZIS-tuhnt) protects against fire

kilowatts (KIH-luh-wahts) a measurement of units of power for an electrical device

modify (MAH-duh-fy) to change something slightly

pole position (POHL puh-ZISH-uhn) the starting position at the front of the starting grid and regarded as the best starting position

qualifying (KWAH-luh-fy-ing) meeting the requirements to be included in a race

status (STA-tuhs) the state or condition of something

Index

ABB FIA Formula E World Championship 18
Anderson, Robert 9
attack mode 17

competition 7, 20, 22, 24, 31
controller 24

helmets 26
pole position 14, 19

steering 24, 25

tires 22, 30
track(s) 6, 9, 14, 17, 18, 27, 28